Off the C

In the vast realm of literature, there are few genres as expressive and captivating as poetry. It serves as a profound medium for delving into the depths of human emotions, offering glimpses into the most intricate aspects of our lives.

In my poetry book "Off the Cuff", I embark on a poetic journey that goes beyond the conventional boundaries of verse. With each line, I explore the realms of politics, asexuality, disability, anxiety, abuse, and my unwavering love for my family.

Through the power of words, I hope to not only evoke emotions, but also spark conversations and ignite change.

I hope you enjoy it.
Daniel 'DK' Kay
2023

Off the Cuff

© Daniel Kay, 2023

The author asserts the moral right under the Copyright, Designs and Patents Act 1988 to be identified as the author of this work.

This edition published by Mini Poetry Press, 2023, www.minipoetrypress.com

ISBN 978-1-916838-36-9

Daniel 'DK' Kay

Off the Cuff

Off the Cuff

Contents

In every heart,
beams equality's pure sunlight,
love's spectrum, it streams

July 8, 2017

July 8, 2017,
    a night to remember
Brother-in-law's folks came by,
    threw logs on the ember
Settled in the living room,
    laughter flowing like a river
Two weeks deep in sobriety,
    I was starting to shiver

Craving hit me like a typhoon,
    feeling so stark
But I held on,
    silent battle in the dark
One drink would be my downfall,
    saw it clear as a spark
So, I stayed on my pathway,
    left my mark

Eyes on the whiskey,
    mirroring a never-ending thirst
Mind reminding me,
    I gotta put my soul first
The pull was insistent,
    like the calling of a lover
But I didn't take a sip,
    didn't let myself hover

Off the Cuff

Held my ground,
   despite the shaking of my core
Reality stared back,
   repeats I can't ignore
Only one way to survive,
   to settle this score
Kept my pledge,
   shut temptation's door

Life continued spinning,
   hour hand ticking
Sound of laughter and clinking
   filled my vision
Sidestepped addiction,
   tightened my conviction
I knew then,
   recovery ain't fiction

That defining night,
   it gave me insight
With a strength from within,
   even in the fight
Not a drop since then,
   continue walking in light
This journey of mine,
   in life's book, I did write

Off the Cuff

Every night,
   confront the demon in the mirror
Walking the sober road,
   vision's getting clearer
In my heart, the truth,
   couldn't be severer
One drink ain't worth the pain...
   it couldn't be dearer

Sober ever since,
   the time has been kinder
Beat addiction's siren,
   now I turn to my grinder
With each sunrise,
   I'm a little bit stronger

Remember that July,
   when I truly wanted a drink
Kept the bottle sealed,
   stood my ground, didn't sink
This is my story,
   I'm an alcoholic no longer

The Mask of Corruption

I need to
   speak my mind
About a subject
   that's got me intertwined
Talking about the government,
   the powers that be
But how can they expect us
   to be corruption-free?

They're playing a game of deception,
   a charade on display
While they're the ones with dirty hands,
   leading us astray
How can they preach morals,
   integrity, and trust
When their pockets are lined
   with bribes and unjust?

It's a double standard they're living,
   a hypocritical stance
Claiming to have our best interests,
   but it's all just a dance
They pass laws and regulations,
   but who really benefits?
It's the ones with power and connections,
   not the average citizen

Off the Cuff

Black lives matter,
   we scream it from the rooftops,
   we won't be ignored
From the streets to the courts,
   we'll fight for what should be restored

I won't conform
   to their greed
I'll rise above
   the system,
plant my own
   righteous seed
I'll light up this darkness
   with the truth I'll reveal
Expose the corruption
   and make them all kneel

In the land
   where Big Ben chimes
   and the tea steeps
Where the people
   demand truth,
   no time for deceit
Prime Minister,
   can't trust his speech
Don't believe his lies,
   he's trying to deceive

Labour, you claim to fight
   for the working class

Off the Cuff

But your actions seem to
   contradict your past
A hypocrite, some say,
   with a hidden agenda
Playing politics,
   like a master pretender

Playing games with our lives,
   while they're counting their stacks
The rich get richer,
   while the poor get taxed
It's a system that's broken,
   it's time to react
We're tired of being pawns
   in their political acts

It's time for us to rise up,
   time for us to fight
Against this corruption,
   against this endless night
We won't be silenced,
   we won't be oppressed
We'll expose their lies,
   we won't settle
   for anything less

Not Just a Label

They say that I'm weak
Because I can't walk or speak
But they don't know the strength
That's hidden within me, deep

I'm not just a label
A diagnosis on a page
I have dreams and desires
And I won't let them fade

I may move slower
But I'm still moving on
I may face challenges
But I know I belong

People underestimate me
Because of what they see
But they don't know my heart
Or the strength I can be

I'm not just a statistic
Or an object of pity
I'm a fighter, a survivor
And I'll rise above this quickly

I'll show the world
What I'm truly made of
Pushing boundaries and limits
With resilience and love

Off the Cuff

I'll shatter stereotypes
And break down any walls
Proving that I am capable
And deserving of it all

So, when you see me
Don't judge me by my chair
See the fire in my eyes
And the greatness I bear

I may have cerebral palsy
But I'm still here to stand
Stronger and more determined
Than they could ever comprehend

I won't be held back
By what others may say
I'll rise to the challenge
And live my life my way

So let them underestimate me
Let them think I can't succeed
For I'll prove them wrong
In everything that I achieve

Hidden Storm

You might not think it, but I have anxiety
A hidden storm that rages deep within me
Behind my smile, a whirlwind of fears
A constant battle that's lasted for years

In crowded rooms, my heart starts to race
An invisible panic, I struggle to erase
The weight on my chest, the breaths that I take
Each moment a battle, each step I must make

Like a garden beneath a vibrant sky
I paint my canvas with a joyful lie
Smiling faces, laughter's sweet embrace
But deep inside, chaos begins to chase

You might not think it,
    but I don't think I'm good enough
Lost in a sea of doubts, swimming in rough
Caught in a storm of insecurities, I find it tough
To believe in myself, to rise above

Everyday tasks become mountains to climb
Simple decisions feel like a crime
I second guess everything that I do
Worrying if I'm good enough,
    if I'll make it through

Off the Cuff

My hands don't shake, but my stomach churns
As my anxiety within me burns
The weight on my chest, it's hard to bear
But I hide it all with a mask of care

I chase after success, fuelled by ambition
But my own expectations bring forth friction
For I set the bar impossibly high
And struggle to touch the sky

I question my worth, my talent, my worthiness
Comparing myself to others,
    feeling endless stress
But deep within me, a fire starts to ignite
A determination to prove myself,
    to shine bright

For beneath the surface,
    a hidden strength resides
A potential waiting to be realised
I may stumble and fall, but I'll rise again
With every setback,
    I'll find the strength to ascend

In the Garden of Innocence

Back in the days when we were young
Playing in the garden, having so much fun
Me and my sister, hand in hand we'd roam
Creating memories, building castles out of stone
Nostalgia hits when I think back now
Those innocent days, how time did allow
Imagination running wild,
    our minds would soar
In that garden, our laughter would always pour

We'd chase butterflies, dance with the flowers
Sunshine on our faces, for hours and hours
Swinging on swings, reaching for the sky
In that garden, time would just fly by
We'd hide and seek, laughter filling the air
As we played together, without a single care
I would wear her "My Little Pony" watch
A token of innocence, a magical touch

And in that magical place, where time stood still
We were just children, with hearts full of thrill
Hand in hand, we'd explore,
    every corner, every nook
Finding hidden treasures,
    like a story from a favourite book
The garden was our haven,
    our sanctuary, our escape
A place where time stood still,

and our souls would reshape
The sun would shine down, warming our skin
As we played and explored, the garden within

We'd build forts with blankets,
   beneath the tall trees
Dreaming of adventures,
   we were unstoppable, nothing could impede
The garden was our sanctuary,
   our secret hideaway
Where we could be ourselves
   and let our dreams sway
We'd talk and we'd share,
   our hopes and our fears
In that garden, we'd wipe away all of our tears
We'd make up games, with rules of our own
Creating memories,
   that would never be outgrown

The games we used to play, in that secret place
In the garden of our youth,
   where time couldn't erase
Every moment filled with joy,
   every second so alive
Oh, how I miss those days, when we were just
kids playing in the garden, side by side

Let Love Ignite

In this cold and heartless world,
    let love take control
A beacon of light,
    let it warm your soul
When the nights get dark,
    and the days grow cold
Embrace the power of love,
    let your heart unfold

Like a fire burning bright, let love ignite
In the darkest of nights, it's your guiding light
No need to fight, just let love unite
Feel the rhythm, let it flow, let it ignite

Let love be the compass,
    leading you on your path
Through the highs and lows, it'll always last
It's a remedy for pain, a remedy for strife
It can heal your wounds
    and bring you back to life

Let love warm your soul,
    let it ignite the fire within
Let it heal your wounds,
    let it wash away your sins
In this chaotic world, let love be your guide
Let it bring you peace, let it be your light

19

Off the Cuff

Just let love in, let it fill your heart
Feel the warmth it brings, like a fiery spark
It can melt away the ice, break down the walls
Open up your mind, let love conquer all

When hatred surrounds you,
    and anger fills the air
Let love be the antidote, let it show you care
When despair overwhelms you,
    and hope seems out of reach
Let love be your anchor,
    the strength that you beseech

When the pressure's on and you're feeling alone
Remember that love can be your cornerstone
It's a power so strong, it can heal any bone
Let it flow through you, let it be known

When darkness engulfs you,
    and shadows cloud your mind
Let love be the light, the beacon you find
When the world seems cold,
    and love feels far away
Let love warm your soul,
    let it brighten your day

For Paul McCartney told me, in a song so wise
That love is the answer, the ultimate prize
So, let go of your worries, let go of your fears
And let love embrace you, wipe away your tears

Freedom and Respect for All

Men, let's take a moment,
   let's have a conversation
About the way we treat women,
   it's time for some contemplation
Bigotry, it's a sickness, a disease
But we can heal it
   if we all agree

Women shouldn't have to ask for Angela,
   that's a fact
They shouldn't have to fear,
   they shouldn't have to react
On a night out, they deserve to feel free
To dance, to laugh, to be who they wanna be

But instead, they're constantly looking
   over their shoulder
Wondering who might approach them
   and make them feel colder
See, it's time we address this aggression
Women shouldn't have to hold
   their keys like a weapon

From the start, we all came from a mother
Ain't it crazy how we sometimes
   forget to love her?
They birthed us all, gave us life
Through pain and sacrifice, they endured strife

21

Off the Cuff

Let them wear heels, let them wear flats
The choice is theirs, let's have their backs
Their safety is important, we all agree
So, let's also give them the freedom to be free

No longer confined to traditional roles
Women are taking charge,
   setting their own goals
Entrepreneurs, leaders, artists, creators
Breaking through barriers, becoming innovators

No more cat calling, no more lewd remarks
They're not objects,
   they're not here for your sparks
They're intelligent, strong,
   and they demand respect
No more being objectified, it's time to reflect

Fellas, check yourselves
   before you wreck yourselves
Time to break free from society's toxic spells
No more feeding into bigotry and hate
Let's elevate, educate, and eradicate

Harmonic Strain

This voice,
   it's from a white man's throat
But it speaks of a culture of which I emote
Raised on hip hop, jazz, and that reggae beat
So Solid Crew, Wiley and Kano,
   UK rap in the 2000s, boy was it sweet

Biggie, Cube, Snoop Dogg, and Tupac,
   they schooled me in the game
Showed me that humanity,
   well, we're all the same
My skin may be light, but my soul understands
The struggles, the triumphs,
   the strength that withstands

Their bars engraved in my memory lane
Not just the rhythm, but the soulful pain
Along came Kendrick with his poetic flame
"Alright" he chants, echoing the same

If you're gripping racism, step out of my light
In a world of colour, only love shines bright
Through rhyme, rhythm,
   the whisper of Mary Jane
We're stitched together,
   in one collective, harmonic strain

Off the Cuff

Grew up in the concrete,
   found my groove in the street
Feel the pulse of reggae,
   my heart repeats the beat
Savouring the flavour of soul food, oh so rich
Life's diverse bounty, ain't that a switch?

The smoke clouds linger, hinting the unknown
A shared perception,
   how understanding has grown
The ink of Lil Wayne flows in my veins
While Dre's beats reverberate in my brain

If you're steeping in prejudice,
   we ain't in the same queue
Life's a vibrant canvas,
   not just monochrome hue
Through bars, beats,
   and the scent of freedom's essence
Unified we stand, diffusing love's fluorescence

So, here's the deal,
   a white man versed in black narratives
Embracing diversity, smashing the preservatives
Never by skin, never by the social decree
It's acceptance, unity, the ties that set us free
Together we dance
   to the rhythm of life's symphony

All Your Lies

You were rosy, a flower in full bloom
But you were plotting and scheming,
    turning evil in the room
You changed like a chameleon,
    flipping your colours
From sweet and innocent to a heartbreaker,
    undercover

Like a wolf in sheep's clothing,
    you were a master of disguise
You had me believing all your lies
Manipulating minds,
    causing chaos and distress
I was blind, I must confess

You played your mind games,
    tried to control me
But I saw through your tricks,
    I ain't nobody's trophy
You tried to make me doubt myself,
    lose my way
But I found my strength,
    now I'm here to stay

You thought you could separate me
    from my family
But little did you know,
    we're tighter than a Grammy

Off the Cuff

You thought you could break me,
   make me weak
But I rose up,
   now I'm standing at my peak

You called my mom a cow, that ain't cool at all
But I won't stoop to your level, gonna stand tall
You said I should stop buying gifts for my sis
But that's just jealousy,
   you were dismissing her bliss

You tried to control me,
   but I wouldn't be contained
I won't let your negativity leave me stained
I rose above, broke free from your grasp
No longer will I let you
   make my happiness collapse

So, keep talking, keep hating, it won't faze me
I'll keep shining bright, living life so free
You may be my ex, but I'm moving on
Leaving you in the past, where you belong

No more fear, no more drama
I'm done with you, no more trauma
I'm stronger now, I've found my voice
I won't let you bring me down; I have a choice

I'm a Rainbow

I'm a rainbow,
    colours bursting through the sky
Shining bright,
    catch me flying oh so high
From red to violet,
    every hue I embody
Spreading love and unity,
    nothing can stop me

I'm asexual,
    but that don't mean I don't feel
The connection, the attraction,
    it's something that's real
I appreciate the beauty,
    the power of the feminine
I admire their strength, their grace,
    it's a feeling within

See, love comes in many forms, it's not just lust
I don't need physical attraction, it's not a must
I'm attracted to their minds, their spirit and soul
It's a connection that runs deep,
    making me whole

I appreciate the beauty in every woman I meet
Their strength, their grace, their power so sweet
It's a love that's platonic, yet so profound
A bond that can't be broken, forever astound

Off the Cuff

I may not feel desire, but I still feel love
A connection so deep, like the stars above
So don't judge me based on
    what you think you know
Asexual love is real, let that truth show

I love women, just not in the sheets
Their grace and strength, they can't be beat
It's the way they hold themselves with pride
Their intelligence and fierce stride

When they walk into a room,
    heads turn, hearts race
Their presence is electric,
    they light up the place
I appreciate their minds,
    their talents, their grace
Women are like a symphony,
    a masterpiece to embrace

So, don't box me in,
    don't judge me by a label
I'm breaking stereotypes,
    I'm unstable
I'm asexual,
    but I love women
Their essence,
    their spirit,
        it keeps me grinning

Sanitary products shouldn't be taxed, because they're not a luxury, and periods are natural. Periods are a natural and normal part of life for billions of women around the world, yet the topic often remains shrouded in silence and shame. It is time we break these barriers and embrace open conversations about menstruation. By educating ourselves and others about periods, we can dispel myths and misconceptions, and empower women to manage their menstrual health with confidence and dignity.

Fighting for Menstrual Equity

Women all around the world,
   you bleed each month
But these extra costs,
   they're really starting to stunt
Your ability to access what you need
   to stay clean
It's time to fight back,
   let's make your voices seen

From the moment that you hit puberty
You're burdened with this monthly duty
Tampons, pads, and other sanitary needs
But why are they treated
   as if they're just weeds?

It's time we acknowledge
   that periods are natural
And make menstrual products

more accessible, it's crucial
Not having access to these products is a shame
Improved access has to be
    the name of the game

Period poverty is real, we must all agree
Let us work together for menstrual equity
Not just for those here, but for women abroad
No woman should face shame,
    it must be outlawed

They say it's just a biological thing
But without these products, life can be a sting
Imagine going through your day,
    feeling unclean
Feeling discomfort,
    like your body's being demeaned

More than just products,
    let's talk about education
Misinformation can lead to undue frustration
To end the stigma,
    we mustn't be afraid to speak
For many, it's an uphill battle, steep and bleak

Women all around the world, it's time to unite
Let us make menstrual access
    every woman's right
From halls of power to streets of every town
Together, let's break every single barrier down

This poem came from a prompt The Word Association sent me as part of their prompt a day. The prompt was "I came from...". So, I wrote this.

Scooby Doo

I came from West Bromwich
A town that always held my heart
Where childhood memories still live
No distance can set us apart

~

My parents raised me with care
My sister a constant friend
My brother-in-law always there
A bond that will never end

~

The streets I used to roam
Played games with friends till the stars shone
Tom and Jerry, Scooby Doo, and
Kim Possible were infused with magic
A world that I relied on

~

Off the Cuff

Morecambe and Wise brought laughter
Victoria Wood's wit was sublime
Julie Walters, the embodiment of strength
Lenny Henry, a master of his time

~

And then there was Muhammad Ali
His spirit larger than life
Michael Jordan in Space Jam
An inspiration through strife

~

These memories filled my youth
With joy and laughter too
They shape the person I am today
A soul forever renewed

They See Me Rolling

They see me rolling, in this wheelchair
Assuming I'm down, like life's unfair
But little do they know, I'm on cloud nine
Living life to the fullest, all the time

I'm breaking stereotypes, shattering the mould
Defying gravity, watch me unfold
I may not walk, but my spirit's free
I'm not defined by this chair, can't you see?

They see me rolling through the streets,
    they stare
But little do they know,
    I'm feeling like a millionaire
While they're busy walking,
    I'm gliding through the crowd
No need for stairs,
    I'm above it all, feeling proud

I'm not confined by the limits they impose
I'm reaching new heights, nobody knows
I'm not limited, I'm limitless, you see
My wheelchair doesn't define the real me

I may be rolling on wheels,
    but my spirit is free
I've learned to rise above,
    and let my passions be

33

Off the Cuff

Don't judge a book by its cover,
   that's what they say
Because I'm here to show you,
   I'm living life my own way

They see my wheels, they think I'm confined
But my spirit's on fire, my soul's defined
I may not walk, but I'm walking tall
No matter what they say, I won't let myself fall

I'm a warrior, fighting battles every single day
Overcoming obstacles,
   I won't let them lead the way
My wheelchair is just a tool,
   it doesn't define my worth
I'm a force to be reckoned with,
   proving my own rebirth

Yeah, they see me rolling in my chair
But little do they know,
   I'm soaring through the air
I may be in a wheelchair,
   but I'm still living my dreams
No limitations,
   I'm breaking
     through
       the seams

Live Life to the Max

I cry on the inside, tears stain my soul
Buried grief within me, trying to stay whole
In this cold world, where emotions collide
I wear a brave face, but I'm hurting deep inside

I pour my heart out on my iPad,
   no censor, just raw
Every lyric, every rhyme,
   a reflection of my flaws
I wear my pain like a badge,
   it's a part of who I am
But society ignores it,
   they don't understand

I grieve on the inside, but I won't let it consume
I wear a smile, but inside I'm in a gloom
Holding back tears, hiding the pain
But my heart's bleeding, like pouring rain

I navigate through life,
   with a poker face
But deep down,
   I'm drowning in a dark space
Every night,
   I lay awake,
     lost in my thoughts
Haunted by the battles that I've fought

Off the Cuff

But I realised, it taught me
   to live life to the Max,
      never compromise
Every day I wake up,
   I cherish the sunrise
Because I know,
   I'll never forget you,
      my friend
Your memory lives on,
   until the very end

Used to drown in sorrow and pain
But now I rise above, like a runaway train
Grief taught me resilience,
   made me stronger than ever
I'm living life to the Max,
   no time for whatever

Every tear shed, a lesson learned
I embrace the pain, it's how I earn
The wisdom and strength to conquer any strife
Grief taught me to appreciate
   every moment of life

I used to dwell in darkness, lost and confused
But now I shine bright, I can choose
Grief taught me to value every breath I take
To chase my dreams, no time to fake

36

In the midst of uncertainty and chaos,
it is crucial to remember...

Everything Will Be Okay

I notice the sunrise, a vibrant display
Painting the sky at the start of the day
But amidst its beauty, my thoughts start to spin
I'm overthinking everything again

I notice the birds, as they swiftly take flight
Their wings spread wide,
   embracing the morning light
But as they soar high, my mind starts to roam
Overanalysing every step I've ever known

I notice the trees, standing tall and strong
Their branches swaying to nature's sweet song
But as they dance, my thoughts become a maze
Lost in worry, consumed by endless ways

I notice the flowers, blooming with grace
Their colours vibrant, bringing joy to this space
But as I admire, my mind begins to wander
Lost in a sea of thoughts, pulled under

I notice the waves, crashing on the shore
Their rhythm soothing, a calming encore
But as they retreat, my mind becomes a storm
Tangled in thoughts, emotions reborn

Off the Cuff

But amidst the chaos, a voice whispers clear
Everything will be okay, there's nothing to fear
I take a deep breath, and I let it all go
Releasing the worries that once plagued me so

I notice the beauty in every moment
    and every scene
In the sunrise, the birds, the trees,
    and the serene
I realise that overthinking only steals my joy
And I have the power to choose a different ploy

I notice the peace that comes with letting go
And embracing the flow of life's ebb and flow
No longer trapped in the prison of my mind
I find solace in the present,
    leaving worries behind

Everything will be okay,
    I remind myself once more
As I open my heart to the beauty
    that lies in store
I notice a sunrise, a vibrant display
And I know that everything will be okay

Revolution is the Solution

Rent spiralling high,
   leaving us with no place to stay
Bills piling up, struggle to make them go away
Minimum wage falls short
   of what we can survive
Stuck in a cycle, feels like a never-ending strive
Politicians discuss "economic growth"
   as if it's the key
Yet all we see is our pockets getting tinier,
   where's the remedy?
Booming economy,
   but who's reaping the benefits?
Certainly not us,
   it's a slap in our face,
     we're not oblivious
We work harder,
   yet what we earn amounts to less
Cost of living continuously oppresses us,
   where's progress?
Changed promised, we're waiting for action
Buried in debt, while they live in mansions
Payday loans are the only option left to survive
It's a vicious cycle, can't help but ask,
   "When will it thrive?"
We're drowning, struggling to put up a fight
Trapped in a never-ending cycle,
   a never-ending plight
Can't even afford meals,

while millionaires grow their stash
It's a daily struggle,
   life feels like a constant crash

Inflation creeps in,
   prices climb higher than most
Cost of living skyrockets,
   a burden we cannot boast
People work two jobs to survive,
   still can't make ends meet
Stripped of necessities,
   a life they cannot delete
The scales must be tipped,
   balance of power must shift
Working-class should no more be victims
   of policies that uplift
Elite and not the people
   they're supposed to serve
Revolution is the solution,
   it's time for them to converge
Rent, bills, inflation, all must be kept in control
We'll fight for our rights, we won't be cajoled
Defeat is not an option,
   we'll struggle with all our might
We won't stop until things are
   as they ought to be, we'll stand and fight

The Love Rainbow's Light

In colours vibrant, a love so alive
Neither in boxes, nor within lines
Different, yet same,
  seeking vivacious vibe
In a world as varied as the vine

Asexual, am I; fond of solace
But, oh, how I cherish the sight
Of people, smiling, in joyous embrace
Underneath the love rainbow's light

Trans women are women, trans men are men
No less, no more, just as they've always been
Their identity, their essence,
  their strength within
It's time to shed bias, remove the unseen

Whether it's he, she, they, or them
Respect the pronouns,
  acknowledge, and see
Beyond the horizons of gender mayhem
Lies the simplicity of human decree

Place no bars on the names we hold dear
Unfolded, transfigured,
  the heart's musings clear
Cherish the names, their echoes, their cheer
For they're the song lines of our life, so near

Off the Cuff

Teach the children, they're sponge ware
The tales of love, courage, and acceptance fair
Whispers of the wind, seeds in the air
Spreading love's message,
    embracing the rainbow flare

Witness the struggle, appreciate the grace
One human to another, it's not a race
A plea for respect, in this vast space
For every colour in the unique embrace

Weaving the world with a phantasm of shades
No room here for hate, only love that pervades
The truth is clear, love is love, it never fades
Seen in the ardour of twilight's cascades

Let us speak and sing in voices, intertwined
For in acceptance, truly, the world's designed
Recite the pledge, of love, unconfined
For in these hearts, we are all intertwined

Tortoise Tempo: Slowing Down the Mind's Race

A mind marathon at play,
    sprinting through boundless space
Tangled thoughts tripping,
    at an unfettered, unruly pace
Thoughts leap so far ahead,
    they begin to fantasise
At my own solemn reprieve,
    with tear-streaked, mournful eyes

On this winding voyage,
    reluctant to meet the finish line
Chasing the shadow of dreams,
    unable to spare the time
Each fleeting second marks the ticking
    of life's grand clock
The need to decelerate evident,
    amidst the turbulent shock

Let wisdom of the tortoise be my guide,
    not the hare's misleading whirl
Embrace the present moment,
    allow such mindfulness to unfurl
Persisting to become an ideal version
    of my existence
Like the tortoise in the race,
    calm and consistent persistence

Off the Cuff

Sometimes, thoughts derailing like
    resolute train off its tracks
The tortoise's timeless wisdom
    my mind vigorously seeks and backs
Progress steady,
    deliberate;
    one measured step at a time
Heed before moving,
    akin to weaving this humble rhyme

In a world of relentless pressure,
    easy is the control we lose
Pursuing every elusive dream,
    that eventually ends in rue
Visions of my funeral,
    haunting, eerily surreal
But today pulsates with life,
    bearing passions still to fulfil

Think like the tortoise,
    not the hare,
    take a weary mental breath
There are burdens to bear,
    adversity to wrestle with,
    till death
Life is a journey,
    not a rapid sprint,
    along its twisted track
Ease the overwhelmed mind,
    cut some plainly deserved slack

Off the Cuff

So, when thoughts begin to race,
   stretching far ahead
Remember the tortoise's tale,
   approach without the dread
Live in the moment,
   suck each minute of its sweet fruit
Life is the journey, not the sprint,
   with you at the root

Channelling the tortoise,
   a renewed state of mind
Eschew stress and kerfuffle,
   serenity to find
Buried the funeral vision deep within the past,
   a mystery
Reclaimed control of my narrative,
   forging my journey's history

With open arms wide,
equality as our guide,
no need to hide, no divide

Thank you
Daniel 'DK' Kay